Schoolwide Discipline Plan
Without the Loopholes

Schoolwide Discipline Plan Without the Loopholes

"Yeah, but... a Salamander

Is Not a Fish!"

Jim Fay

Love and Logic Institute, Inc.

2207 Jackson Street, Golden, CO 80401-2300

www.loveandlogic.com

800-338-4065

LOVE AND LOGIC, LOVE & LOGIC, BECOMING A LOVE AND LOGIC PARENT, AMERICA'S PARENTING EXPERTS, LOVE AND LOGIC MAGIC, 9 ESSENTIAL SKILLS FOR THE LOVE AND LOGIC CLASSROOM, and
are registered trademarks or trademarks of the Institute For Professional Development, Ltd. and may not be used without written permission expressly granted from the Institute For Profession Development, Ltd.

 Published and printed in the United States of America

Library of Congress Cataloging-in-Publication Data

Fay, Jim.
  "A salamander is not a fish!" : a positive schoolwide discipline plan without the loopholes / Jim Fay.
      p. cm.
  Includes bibliographical references and index.
    ISBN 1-930429-75-4 (alk. paper)
   1. School discipline--United States. 2. School children--United States--Discipline. 3. Classroom management--United States. I. Title.
LB3012.2.F38 2005
371.5--dc22

                            2004029658

About the Author

THE LEGENDARY JIM FAY began his career as a teacher, and for over three decades served in public, private, and parochial schools. He spent seventeen years as a school principal and administrator, and for nearly thirty years has served as an educational consultant and public speaker.

Jim's teaching experience in both inner city and suburban schools revealed a need to structure the educational environment in a way that would build positive relationships with students. This structure also had to address the need to teach children responsibility and self-discipline, and at the same time keep educators from being labeled as "mean." To meet this need, Jim devised the Love and Logic technique for use in both homes and classrooms.

One of Jim's goals is to give educators the skills they need to return home at the end of the day with energy left over for themselves and their families. Because of his experience and ability to help educators, Jim has won many awards in the education field.

Project Coordinator: Carol Thomas

Editing by Jason Cook, Denver, CO

Cover design and interior design by Michael Snell,
Shade of the Cottonwood, Topeka, KS

Published and printed in the United States of America.

Contents

Introduction

By Bob Sornson, Ph.D.

I visited a great school recently. After more than thirty years of going in and out of schools, it only takes me a few minutes to notice which schools have a culture of respectful behaviors, which support great learning and teaching. It was toward the end of the school day when I arrived. As I walked in, a little second-grade girl who was struggling with her coat met my eyes. She paused and smiled, then refocused on the task of getting her coat on before locating her backpack. The hallway hummed with the noise of purposeful activity. A teacher was offering small encouragements to the children. She bore the look of a master craftsperson, connected to her work, carefully watching the flow of activity around her. Then she greeted me and directed me to the office.

It's the little things that tell the story. The clean halls filled with displays of children's work, the harmony of synchronous sounds, more love than stress, more purpose than anxiety, a sense of connection between people.

In the great modern rush to improve schools by raising test scores we may be overlooking some basic truths. Children learn best when they feel safe, valued, and successful. Teachers teach best when they feel safe, valued, and successful.

Many schools have responded to the pressure of the modern age by increasing the content of the curricula and the rigidity of the student code.

Both educators and students feel the pressure. Some become overwhelmed by the pressure.

Love and Logic is not designed to solve all the issues that are associated with the push for accountability and greater achievement. But it is a philosophy that helps us thoughtfully approach the challenge of turning good schools into great schools.

Love and Logic helps us create the relationships and respectful environments that are at the heart of great learning communities. The bottom line is that Love and Logic is a tool that makes what we do easier and better.

For those of you who are considering this path, let me say in advance that Love and Logic is not a lockstep system. Instead it is a philosophy, a way of thinking respectfully about self and others, that offers a menu of highly effective skills with which you can experiment. This book will describe the ideas and skills that can help you embrace this path. It uses stories to illustrate ideas, and encourages you to practice your way to becoming a Love and Logic master educator.

To help you choose between Love and Logic and the tendency to discipline with warnings, threats, intimidation, and complex regulation, consider the following principles and beliefs you will find along the Love and Logic path:

- Adults are responsible for setting limits in the school, in a respectful and empathetic way.
- Mistakes are wonderful opportunities for important learning.
- Children and adults work and learn best in a place where they feel physically and emotionally safe.
- Children need practice in problem solving if they are to develop powerful problem-solving skills for life.
- Practicing habits of respectful behavior toward others is a valuable habit for life.
- Practicing setting appropriate limits on how you allow others to treat you is a valuable habit for life.
- Strength is developed when struggling toward a meaningful goal.

- People have different learning needs, strengths, and goals. These differences deserve our respect. Treating all people the same when teaching or managing behavior is seldom respectful.
- Self-efficacy is developed by thousands of experiences of giving sincere effort and achieving success.
- The paths toward greatness are followed because of a deep, intrinsic desire.
- Our goal in schools is to create confident, purposeful, lifelong learners who find pleasure in meaningful effort.
- Great schools are catalysts for great learning among students, staff, and parents.
- Relationships and trust are the foundation of a learning community.
- Great teachers weave the elements of great learning into a caring classroom, avoid coercive behavior, and carefully train themselves to adjust their own responses to help students be successful.
- Great teachers see the miracle in every child, find the strengths in every person, and expect great things from everyone they teach.

The path of Love and Logic helps teachers create conditions that are absolutely essential for great academic and social learning. Whenever possible, consider finding friends and asking for support along the way. Make plenty of mistakes, and laugh when you notice them. Practice, practice, practice. And find meaning by helping children and their families develop the strengths, skills, and beliefs that allow us all to build a better future.

I am honored to write the introduction for this significant contribution to education by the legendary Jim Fay.

Bob Sornson, Ph.D.
Executive Director of Special Services
Northville Public Schools

"A Salamander Is Not a Fish!"

This is a book about students who make educators fantasize about self-destructive acts such as pulling out clumps of their own hair and early retirement. These are the students who don't respond to traditional discipline plans. They are diabolic in their abilities to demonstrate that rules and consequences don't apply to them. The impression they exude is, "You can't control me with your stupid rules and consequences—I don't care what you do."

Curt was one of these kids. He attended a middle school that was ruled by a traditional discipline plan. The school staff had developed a list of rules that appeared to address every possible negative behavior ever thought of by young adolescents. Each rule was followed by a sequence of consequences, with increasing severity ranging from a first offense, consisting of a warning, to the tenth offense, which was expulsion from school.

The staff's thinking was that if kids knew in advance what would happen, they would be motivated to behave out of fear of the prescribed consequences. And if they did violate the rules, the kids and their parents knew in advance exactly what would happen.

The staff also believed that this would create consistency of staff reactions. Every child would be treated exactly the same. Therefore, parental complaints about fairness would no longer be a problem. This approach seemed to make sense and it was similar to what was being done in many schools in America.

Curt and his parents were well aware of the discipline policy, and both had signed off on their understanding of it.

As with many chronic offenders, Curt felt a responsibility to test the policy. One day he teasingly slapped a girl up the side of her head with a dead fish as they passed in the hallway. True to form, he did this within eyesight of the hall supervisor, who immediately announced, "Hey, that's against the rules. You're going to the office!"

Curt cooperatively went to the office to await a reprimand from the principal. And then heard the same thing: "That's against the rules. You can't behave that way at this school. I'm assigning you to in-school suspension for one full day."

"What rule?" asked Curt. "I didn't violate none of your rules. Me and my dad read all the rules in that Student Conduct Policy. I counted them up. There are eighty-seven rules in this school and not one of them says anything about fish. It's not fair. Besides, this is my first offense about fish and the policy says I'm just supposed to get a warning on any first offense."

"Of course there's no rule about fish," said the principal. "We haven't needed one in the past, but what you're doing is disruptive and you're still going to serve a day of in-school suspension."

"Okay, I'll do it, but this is so stupid. I was just having some fun. It didn't hurt nobody!"

Sad to say, the Student Conduct Policy was revised within days of this incident. There are now 248 rules in that school, including one about fish.

Two weeks later Curt teased the same girl by rubbing something dead and slimy in her hair. Ironically, he did it in front of the same hall supervisor. Curt was once more sent to the office. However, this time he stopped at his locker to pick up an encyclopedia that he had brought from home. He had highlighted excerpts in advance so that when he showed it to the principal he could say, "See, it says right here that a salamander is not a fish, and your new rule says 'fish.'"

This true story is one of the more outrageous examples I've heard in my long experience with schools. But it does a great job of illustrating the futility of attempting to control student behavior with traditional prescriptive discipline plans that have long lists of rules and consequences.

Before we get into the meat of this book, I feel a strong need to make it clear that schools need structure. Structure provides security for students and staff. Rules that are enforced provide the foundation for this structure. The Love and Logic approach outlined in this book does not, in any way, encourage permissiveness.

With this book, I will provide an alternative to the use of prescriptive discipline plans. The method is tried and true. It is practical and easy to implement. Better yet, it does not catch staff members in the kind of bind experienced by this child's principal. The method will provide the flexibility needed to address any and all kinds of behaviors, even those not yet designed by chronic offenders such as Curt.

The school staff in this example fell into a trap of their own making. In their attempts to provide structure and consistency, as well as protect themselves from parental complaints about fairness, they produced a prescriptive discipline plan that attempted to address all possible breaches of conduct by the students. Some have labeled this a "cookbook" approach to discipline.

Many schools and school districts have adopted this approach. Their plans vary in creativity. Some are huge legal documents that spell out all the rights and responsibilities of students and their parents. These often include the legal rights of special needs students as well as alternative school participants, and spell out procedures to be followed in the event of legal challenges to disciplinary action. At the other end of the continuum are discipline plans that are far less legal in nature.

Regardless of the complexity or simplicity of these plans, they still list rules and prescribe consequences. In recent years there has also been a movement to make prescribed consequences progressive in nature. Each successive breach of conduct earns the student a more severe punishment.

Prescriptive discipline plans are like tiger traps set in a jungle path. Everything on the surface looks good from eye level, but what looks like a solid path suddenly gives way, leaving a large hole from which there is no escape. To help educators avoid these traps, we must first examine the invalid beliefs that form the foundation of these prescriptive discipline plans.

Trapped in My Own Invalid Beliefs

How many schools have fallen into the trap of believing the following:

• If kids knew exactly what kind of consequences they would face when rules are broken, they would not break the rules.
• If kids continue to break the rules, it is because either
    a. the consequences are not severe enough,
    b. the administrators and the other teachers must not be enforcing the consequences as prescribed in the discipline plan, or
    c. the administrators must be letting parents rescue the kids from the consequences.

If these beliefs were true, discipline would not be a problem in most schools. Many school discipline plans are developed around the idea that kids and parents should know exactly how each rule violation will be treated. I have actually seen school discipline plans where there are five different consequences spelled out for each rule infraction so that students face increasingly severe consequences each time the rule is violated

I once witnessed a situation in which a student had been referred to the principal over twenty times. He had never received more than a warning because he was smart enough to violate a different rule each time. When the principal finally decided to give a more severe consequence, the parents argued that he was not following the discipline policy, and was therefore discriminating against their child.

Discipline plans that lock in or prescribe consequences are psychologically unsound. They violate a psychological principle known as the "Threat Cycle." The Threat Cycle was well researched and documented by Dr. Raymond Wlodkowski in the early 1970s when he was professor of psychology at the University of Wisconsin. Similar research was conducted by J. W. Brehm, who developed the theory of "Psychological Reactance." Brehm's research taught us that perceived threats to freedom are met with behaviors designed to regain a sense of control.

It should be remembered that threats appear to work well with the population of kids who don't need them. This can explain how adults get tricked into believing that threats should work on the chronically disruptive students. However, threats tend to scare naturally well-behaving kids and eat away at their sense of security and good feelings about the school.

Have you ever known people who are intimidated by threats? Sure you have. Threats work on just enough people that we get tricked into believing that threats should work on everyone. Unfortunately, many people view a threat as the possible loss of control. Loss of control is scary for humans, since control is one of our basic needs.

Human beings react to loss of control with a fight or flight response. This reaction takes different forms in different people, but is usually manifested by one of the following:

a. passive-aggressive behaviors
b. passive-resistive behaviors
c. overt aggression

We have all seen threats backfire, providing the wrong kind of power to the student who was threatened. Consider Janice, a student who was warned that one more outburst in class would result in her being excluded from the class party. Of course she had to test this limit. Her teacher followed through with her threat and Janice sat in the office while the other kids had their party.

Now, did Janice sit in the office saying to herself, "I was really stupid ... I'm really going to get my behavior straightened out ... I'm going to be a good girl from now on ... I learned my lesson"? What a joke. We know she didn't do that.

The advance warning about this consequence gave her plenty of time to convince herself that she didn't want to go to that stupid party after all. She probably spent her time thinking that she was lucky not to be involved in something as lame as a class party. Of course she reserved some of her time to think up nasty names for her teacher and to become more resentful.

Challenging kids feel a responsibility to test our warnings and threats. It is possible to actually set these kids up to misbehave.

Before offering an alternative to prescriptive discipline plans it is important to examine what is known about the kids who create the necessity for discipline plans. These are the repeat offenders, the kids who habitually misbehave and appear to be unaffected by disciplinary actions.

Some Chronically True Facts About Chronically Disruptive Students

Are there some kids who live to please their teachers? And are there others who make a hobby out of predicting what their teaches want, so they can do the opposite? With which students do traditional discipline plans—those based on rules, threats, and warnings—work? Let's first consider some basic assumptions of these approaches.

Invalid Assumptions About Chronically Disruptive Students

- Difficult students behave only when they know exactly what the adults in their lives want. We post rules so these kids will know what we want them to do.
- Difficult students behave only when they know exactly what will happen to them if they break the rules. That's why we must warn them of the specific consequences they'll experience if they misbehave.
- The key to getting difficult kids to behave is to find consequences that scare them enough to keep them from breaking the rules.

With these assumptions in mind, let's consider some key questions. Which kids walk into the classroom on the first day of class, spot the teacher's list of rules, and think, "That's what my teacher doesn't want me to do ... I better not upset her"? In contrast, which kids spot the rules and think, "That's what my teacher doesn't want me to do ... Now I know exactly what will turn her face red ... This is going to be great"?

After being warned of consequences, which kids reason, "I sure wouldn't want that to happen"? Which kids receive the very same warnings and think, "I bet I can break the rules in such a way that the consequences won't fit ... Then I'll get some practice for the Bar exam by arguing the fairness of my case ... Besides, even if I'm not acquitted, the consequence will be a wonderful badge of honor with my friends ... They'll finally see how cool I am"?

Which kids really fear the consequences we are legally able to provide? Which kids are facing much scarier things—such as domestic violence, abuse, gang warfare, divorce and custody battles, poverty, parents who spoil them so badly that they have no skills and no self-esteem, etc.—in their homes and neighborhoods on a daily basis?

We often joke that discipline plans based upon threats and fear of punishment work only with the kids who don't need threats and fear of punishment, or the really well-behaved kids. This isn't entirely accurate. The following is closer to the truth:

Discipline plans based upon threats and fear of punishment are worse than worthless. They scare the well-behaved kids and prove to the chronically disruptive ones that we are powerless.

I've never met an educator who saw value in scaring the most well-behaved students. It doesn't take a Ph.D. to see the silliness in this.

Sadly, I've met a few educators who believe that scaring poorly behaved students is the only way to make them behave and learn. A closer look at the characteristics shared by chronically disruptive youngsters shows why threats, warnings, and other scare tactics backfire.

Characteristics of Chronically Disruptive Students

Chronically disruptive students see life as a win/lose control battle.

Responsible kids who feel good about themselves also feel good about complying with our wishes, and the rules we set. They view life as a win/win proposition. They feel pretty much in control of their own lives, so they feel pretty good about sharing control with others. For them, rule-following is a breeze. If they give adults what they want, adults feel good too. Everybody wins.

A much different state of affairs exists for challenging children who feel poorly about themselves. Since they feel out of control most of the time, they hoard control by refusing to give others what they want. While clearly self-defeating in the long term, this approach gives them a fleeting sense of being in charge of their lives. Living by their tough kid logic, they reason, "If I follow the rules and give my teacher what he wants, he will win and I will lose. If I make him happy, I'll be unhappy. No way is he gonna get what he wants!"

Chronically disruptive students only respect those who back up their words with actions.

When we post rules, such as "keep your hands to yourself," "treat others with respect," or "be quiet when I am teaching," are we actually promising something we cannot deliver? Of course we are. These are all unenforceable statements.

It takes approximately one millisecond for a challenging child to look at a traditional list of rules and think, "Big deal. They can't make me!"

Here's the problem: The child is right. Short of employing barbaric or illegal tactics, we can't make another human being keep their hands to themselves, treat others with respect, be quiet, or do anything else.

As soon as rules such as these are broken—regardless of any consequence we may deliver—it's already too late. The student has just proven to him- or herself, and everyone else, that we are powerless to control them.

There are few things more exciting to a chronically disruptive student than witnessing an entertaining display of adult frustration or anger. Chronically disruptive kids are addicted to unhealthy control. Nothing gives them a greater sense of power over the adults in their lives than seeing that they can control the color of our faces, the tone and volume of our voices, and the prominence with which the veins on our foreheads pulse.

Discipline plans based on threats and fear of punishment lead to inevitable power struggles that simply cannot be won. As these battles wage, the most difficult kids in our lives develop an even greater addiction to the thrill of fighting them. Quite simply, there is nothing that feeds misbehavior more than kids seeing adults get angry and frustrated.

Chronically disruptive students tend to interpret the actions of others as hostile.

Sound psychological research has shown that angry and oppositional kids have highly attuned "threat detectors." Through their eyes, they see most people as being out to get them. Most educators can attest to this by the number of times they have asked a student why a fight started and got the answer, "I had to, man. He looked at me."

Healthy kids do not read hostility into a look. Yet kids who feel poorly about themselves misread a look as hostility or aggression. Through their eyes, they see most people as being out to get them. Discipline plans based on threats and fear of punishment feed directly into this unhealthy view of the world. Instead of guiding them to eventually perceive the adults in their lives as allies, these discipline plans verify the following malignant mythology:

My teachers are always on my case. Everybody's always on my case! They don't care. They just get off on bossing kids around.

Healthy people are fooled by their own healthy view of the world.

Here's the rub. Well-meaning healthy adults who see the world as a win/win place do not view prescriptive discipline plans as threatening. They tend to view describing warnings about possible consequences as a way of helping kids avoid the inconvenience of making bad choices. Challenging kids, in contrast, see warnings about consequences as highly threatening. The degree of threat perceived by the child is directly proportional to his or her poor self-concepts and negative life experiences.

Chronically disruptive students tend to act out when exposed to chronically controlling adults.

Gasoline, paint thinner, turpentine, fireworks, dynamite—the packaging on all of these items contains a warning: "Keep away from fire, flame, or extreme heat." Unfortunately, there are some teachers and other adults working in the schools who are like fire, flame, or extreme heat. These folks really *do* "get off" on bossing kids around. They would rather bark orders than build the kind of relationships with kids that encourage co-operation.

Discipline plans based on threats and fear of punishment actually encourage these chronically disruptive staff members in our schools to behave in ways that feed the fire.

The only effective motivator for chronically disruptive students is a positive relationship with a significant adult.

It's time for some stories.

"Nobody Can Make Me Stay In School!"

Fifteen-year-old Marcus had a problem. He hated his teachers, he hated his school, and he hated waiting for the bell to ring. The slightest provocation or perceived insult would lead Marcus to rise prominently from his seat, proclaim disdain for the current lesson plan, walk out of class, and keep going. One of his peers, whose mother was quite the Elvis fan, would remark upon his exit, "Marcus has now left the building."

This was no joking matter for the adults who cared deeply about Marcus. They tried all the typical techniques to solve the problem:

- Lecture him about the importance of getting a good education and about how hard it is to make it in the real world without one.
- Remind him that he is wasting his potential.
- Warn him that he will earn in-school suspension if he leaves class.
- Give him three days of in-school suspension.
- Say to him that he might be taken off of the basketball team if he continues to behave this way.
- Warn him that he will receive out-of-school suspension if this continues.
- Give him two days of out-of-school suspension.
- Assign Saturday School (which he also walked out on).

Nothing seemed to work until one of his teachers took a completely different tact. She used a Love and Logic technique called the "One-Sentence Intervention." Two or three times a week, she'd spot Marcus in the hall, mosey up to him, smile, and whisper something positive yet very brief. Each time she noticed just one of the following:

> "I noticed that you like basketball."
> "I noticed that you like the LA Lakers."
> "I noticed you guys talking about Magic Johnson."
> "I noticed that you don't let anybody push you around on the court."
> "I noticed that you've grown about three inches since the beginning of the year."
> "I noticed that your shoes are about twice as long as mine. Where do you buy ones that big?"

About a month into her new approach, the fire alarm went off for a drill. As she led her students outside, she thought, "Marcus won't hesitate to use this as an excuse to leave early."

As everyone waited outside the building, it appeared that her prediction had sadly come true. Marcus was nowhere to be seen. As she led her class back inside after the drill, she couldn't help but feel saddened that yet another technique had failed. Or had it?

She felt a soft tap on the back as she entered the room. Turning around, she saw Marcus, smiling from ear to ear. "I bet you thought I left, Teach," was all he said.

From that day on, she was the one teacher who could keep Marcus in class. And from that day on, she realized what all great teachers know:

There will never be enough consequences to motivate tough kids to learn and to behave if we are not first developing positive relationships. And without positive teacher-student relationships, no discipline plan will work.

The Sunglasses Saga

Jim was raring to go. He'd attended a Love and Logic seminar and had some new skills to try out. And he was getting his first long-term substitute job at the local high school.

He'd been "wired" as he waited for the seminar to end so he could tell me that he had a goal of teaching for an entire week without getting into the Threat Cycle with a student.

"Wow, Jim," I said. "That's great. What are you going to be teaching?"

"I'm going to be teaching a poetry unit to tenth-graders."

"Uh, oh," I thought. "He may be in for a surprise about how excited tenth-grade boys are about the combination of poetry and substitute teachers." But I kept these concerns to myself.

As you might guess, he got the baptism of fire. As he and the other teachers waited in the main hall they spied Jack, one of the tougher students, sauntering in, sporting a new set of outrageous sunglasses. Instead of having glass lenses in them they had louvers.

The first-hour teacher declared the glasses "disruptive to the educational process" and immediately accosted the teen: "Take those off your face. You're not wearing those in my classroom."

"Say what? I can wear these if I want. They're not hurtin' nobody!"

"I say that they're disruptive, now take them off!"

"You want them off, man? You try and take 'em off. I'm wearing 'em unless you think you're man enough to take 'em from me."

Needless to say, the teacher backed down and Jack wore the glasses. But the second-hour teacher had witnessed this episode and braced himself for a showdown. When Jack showed up at this teacher's door he was met with, "Don't take another step into this room until you lose those glasses."

Jack was also ready to raise the ante, muttering, "You ever hear of the ACLU, man? I think my rights are being violated." Jack continued to wear the glasses.

Having witnessed these interchanges, Jim, who planned to teach for an entire week without getting into the Threat Cycle with a student, was rifling through his Love and Logic course book. The only possibility appeared to be the One-Sentence Intervention technique, which suggested "I noticed ..." statements similar to those used in the previous story. His immediate concern was that he didn't have time to notice a variety of things. He had to act now.

Meeting Jack at the door, Jim said, "Hey!"

"What!"

"Are those boots custom made?"

"What?"

"Are those boots custom made?"

"No, man. These came from K-Mart. Anybody can get 'em. They're only thirty-nine dollars."

"Well, I noticed those." And with that Jim walked away. Then this skillful teacher turned back toward Jack with an almost distracted manner and asked, "Oh, by the way, would you consider ... I mean, would you consider not wearing those glasses just while you're in my room? Thanks." And with that he turned his back and went toward his desk.

"Man, I just don't know what the big deal is with these glasses," grumbled Jack as he jammed them into his pocket and threw himself into his seat.

The other teachers who'd watched this couldn't wait to meet Jim in the lounge to find out what he's said that had worked so well with that tough kid. When they asked, Jim just said, "Oh, nothing much. I just told him that I was going to kick his rear if he didn't do what I told him to."

When I asked Jim why he hadn't told them that a genuine concern for relationship and talking with respect was the secret to gaining co-operation, he responded with, "Ah, they believe the only way to work with tough kids is to out-tough them. They wouldn't have believed me if I had told them the truth "

When I asked Jim what this experience had taught him, he replied, "I now understand why you taught us that we must share control if we are to gain control. The first two teachers attempted to take total control, and ended up having none. I left Jack a small measure of control and I was rewarded with some, myself.

"Besides, we both had retained some respect. I didn't order him to take them off. I simply asked him if he would *consider* taking off the glasses. If he didn't agree, I had nothing to lose. I could have thanked him for considering it for me. I'd still be a winner. Those other teachers could only win if he obeyed. There was no way he could win. They set up their own win/lose situation."

Either we give control on our terms or others take it on their terms.

The most effective teachers give away two kinds of control: the control they don't absolutely need, and the control they never had in the first place.

Two Approaches to School Discipline

What provides the guiding light for your school? Is it a set of basic principles, or a set of rules? As we move toward our goal of providing an alternative to prescriptive discipline plans, this chapter is devoted to examining two different approaches to schoolwide discipline. The first school is typical of many in America. Discipline is based upon a system. In this school the teachers apply disciplinary actions that are presented by a system developed by a discipline committee.

The second school's approach to discipline is based upon a set of basic principles shared by the staff. In this school the teachers create disciplinary actions that are consistent with a set of basic principles developed and agreed upon by the entire staff.

Attica High School

The principal was frustrated yet another time. Mr. Blackendekker, the industrial arts teacher, was complaining that he didn't have enough discipline in his class—he'd have more if the other teachers would just follow the discipline plan the way they were supposed to.

"Of course I was yelling at Festus. It's the only thing he understands. He comes into my classroom all wired up because the other teachers let him get by with everything. Why should he think he has to be any better when he comes to my room? He knows the principal is not going to back me up.

"I shouldn't even have to be spending my time when they act up. I'm here to teach, not to baby-sit these kids. Then I send them to you for some discipline and what happens? Nothing! The parents complain and you back down and give the kids another chance. No wonder we have discipline problems at this school."

Understandably, the principal is frustrated because there is a measure of truth in what Mr. Blackendekker is saying. This makes it difficult for him to get this teacher to look at his own discipline skills as a possible source of the problem. Mr. Blackendekker has taken an offensive position, leaving the principal in a defensive position.

Mr. Blackendekker is blaming everyone else for his problems with kids. The present schoolwide discipline policy has provided him with all the excuses he needs. His major excuse is that the teachers at Attica High are not consistent. They are not consistently supporting each other and they do not respond in manners consistent with the prescribed set of consequences spelled out under the discipline policy. He can blame everyone else for his problems.

This shows the typical problems with prescriptive discipline policies. They have some fatal flaws. One of these flaws is a belief that all teachers will view student behavior in the same way. Therefore it should be possible to expect every teacher to respond in a consistent manner.

But is this true? Do any two people view the world exactly the same? Isn't it more likely that we all view the world in different ways based upon our past experiences and our inborn temperaments?

Two teachers, Sally and Veronica, are walking down the hall. They see a student, Jackie, running down the hall. Sally thinks to herself, "Jackie's in a hurry. She's trying to get to class on time." At the same time Veronica is thinking to herself, "Look how bad that kid is behaving. I'd better get her straightened out before all the other kids start thinking it's okay to run." Isn't this human nature?

Now, my question to you is: How likely is it that those two teachers are going to respond in a consistent manner to the rule that prohibits running in this school? And I ask yet another question: What are the odds that fifty different staff members could all view student behavior in exactly the same way, and therefore react the same way, providing consistent discipline?

The fallacy in this is easy to see. Unfortunately, a belief that all teachers should respond in a consistent manner to misbehaving students is the foundation for many schoolwide discipline plans. Is it any wonder that these discipline plans fail to meet expectations? Buildings that are constructed on weak foundations soon crack and deteriorate. Discipline policies are no different.

Behavior management at Attica High remains a problem since it is based upon a "cookbook" approach.

Two Approaches to School Discipline

Cookbook Approach

Rules are developed.

Students are expected to follow the rules.

Staff members meet to create a set of punishments or consequences for violations. These are established and published in advance in a sequential manner. Everyone knows what is going to happen for the first offense, second offense, third offense, etc.

All staff members are expected to impose punishments in a manner consistent with the cookbook discipline plan.

Typical Results

Staff members who have difficulty dealing with students often blame it on the fact that others are not enforcing the rules consistently. It is common to hear, "I wouldn't be having this trouble if the others would just enforce the rules the way they should!"

Staff members often complain that others allow the students to get away with infractions. The staff often becomes fragmented or polarized. Staff morale is often low.

There are frequent concerns that punishments don't quite fit the offenses.

Many staff members ignore infractions because they do not agree with the prescribed set of punishments or consequences.

Students often use this to their advantage and manipulate the adults.

The staff cries for more rules and more consistency.

Numerous complaints about teachers and students.

Principles-Based Approach

Rules are developed and posted.

Students are expected to follow the rules.

Staff members are expected to enforce the rules and take action when rules are violated.

Staff members meet to agree upon a common set of principles, which serve as the basis for all decisions regarding the treatment of discipline problems.

Consistency is achieved when discipline situations are handled in a manner consistent with an agreed set of principles. Recognizing that it is almost impossible to achieve total consistency of beliefs and reactions within a staff, teachers are encouraged to discipline students by selecting from a range of consequences with the understanding that the consequence or counseling used is consistent with the set of values or principles commonly agreed upon by the staff as a whole.

Typical Results

Staff members are neither allowed nor encouraged to blame their problems on the techniques used by others. It is understood that each person will develop special relationships with children and that these will be different in every case.

This leaves staff members with the responsibility of learning how to respond to students and set limits in effective ways rather than expecting others to do it for them.

Staff members find a need to develop a range of consequences that can be used in different situations according to the severity of the infraction.

Teachers feel like professionals.

Notice that in the cookbook plan there are frequent concerns about consistency. The frequent cry is, "If everyone else would just enforce the rules on a consistent basis, we wouldn't be having so many discipline problems." On the surface this appears to make sense. However, if different people see things in different ways, there will never be consistency between human responses. This view of consistency often pits staff members against each other and can be a severe source of morale problems.

Consistency

> **Where do we find consistency—between people,**
> **or between people and principles?**

The *form* that consistency takes is the essential element in a discipline program. Instead of insisting that staff members agree on a prescribed response, there need only be agreement that misbehavior will not be ignored and that basic principles will be adhered to. The staff agree to deal with each misbehaving student in a manner that seems appropriate, given the unique aspects of the situation.

Some of you will be surprised by this. The Love and Logic philosophy actually assumes that teachers and administrators and all frontline people can actually think for themselves! I understand that this is a rather radical thought (sarcasm intended) in our present political climate. However, my vast experience says that educators can and do become quite capable of quality thought when given the latitude. I have encountered too many teachers and administrators who feel forced to adhere to prescribed reactions from their policy books instead of doing what is best for the individual child.

It's time for another true story.

Mooning the Class

Mark was a first-grader with limited social skills. As part of his ongoing quest for attention he pulled his pants down. With a graceful pirouette, he exposed first his back-side and then his front-side to the class. His angry teacher immediately sent for the principal and removed Mark from the class. By the time he arrived in the office he was obviously embarrassed by what he did and was crying for forgiveness.

Mark's school was governed by a typical discipline plan that prescribed a three-day suspension for this kind of behavior. Mark's parents were called and he was immediately taken home.

"What's wrong with this?" you ask. His behavior was outrageous and deserving of a serious consequence. The principal supported his staff by following the discipline plan to the letter.

The principal of this school understood kids and their behavior. He told me later that a far more effective consequence would have been for Mark to be sent back to class to face the other kids while he was still embarrassed about what he had done. He wanted to simply put his arm around Mark and say, "I'm disappointed in your choice of expression. Now head back and face the class. Try not to be too embarrassed." Sending him home gave him a chance to escape the true natural consequences of his acts. Better yet, three days away from school gave him plenty of time to forget and made it much easier to face the class.

Sad, but true, this is one more example of prescribed consequences getting in the way of doing what is right and best for kids. If this school had been governed by a principles-based approach to discipline, the principal would have had both the freedom and the responsibility to deal with this situation in a more effective way.

A school discipline plan must provide opportunities to do what is most effective and best for each unique situation, and for each unique child.

Consistency means that when there is a problem, it will be addressed; and that when there is misbehavior, it will be addressed.

Consistency does not mean that everyone will react in the same way.

Same Is Not Always Fair or Equal

I've had the honor and luxury of presenting to large audiences in many states. This gives me the opportunity to ask questions and discover how groups of parents and teachers think and feel about kids.

For teacher audiences one of my favorite prompts goes like this: "You get to choose a school for your own kids. Raise your hands if you choose a school where everyone gets treated the same. Raise your hands if you choose a school where your child is treated as a unique individual." I can always predict the vote. All hands go up voting for the school where children are treated as unique individuals.

Now I can have some fun with the audience. "If this is the way you would vote, how do you think nonteacher parents would vote?" They audience agrees that all parents would probably feel the same.

"Good," I say. "Now, when do you think you will get the most support from the community? Will it be when you tell the community that your school staff treats every kid and every situation the same, or will it be when you say that kids in your school are treated as individuals and discipline problems are handled on a case-by-case basis?" The answer to this question is always the same. The vote of the audience is, "We'd probably get the most support from parents when they know that their children will be treated as unique individuals."

I love to follow this up with, "Oh, by the way, do you know any schools where all kids are treated exactly the same way?" The teachers are quick to admit that this does not happen, for many reasons. This gives me a chance to ask the final question: "Do you know any schools that lie about it and claim that every kid and every discipline situation gets treated the same?" The audience gets rather quiet at this point.

Of course, most people in the audience have never thought about their prescriptive discipline plan as a purposeful attempt to mislead the community. They created prescriptive discipline plans to eliminate possible complaints about unfair treatment of students.

This series of questions makes it easy for educators to get a clearer focus on ways to better reach kids and their parents, namely treating misbehavior and/or discipline on a case-by-case basis.

Experts remind us that a thoughtful and professional reaction to misbehavior requires consideration of several factors, what we call the *Five Critical Disciplinary Considerations:*

1. The precipitating events.
2. The child's intentions.
3. The personality and temperament of the child.
4. What actually happened.
5. The damage or hurt caused by the misbehavior or rule violation.

Prescriptive discipline plans fail to address all of these issues.

Put yourself in the position of a middle school principal. You are required to decide appropriate consequences for two youngsters, seventh-grader Judy and Jan, another student whom Judy bickered with yesterday. "I'm going to get you tomorrow!" Judy screamed. "I'll cut your ugly face and you'll be sorry you ever messed with me!"

One of the teachers broke up this argument, and as a result was on the lookout for weapons. Today she caught Judy threatening Jan with the knife. The knife was confiscated and Judy was escorted to your office. Judy is waiting in the outer office for her meeting with you.

After dealing with Judy you will need to meet with Sheila. She is also accused of possessing a dangerous weapon. She had planned to go directly to the church youth group meeting from school today. The girls were planning to make care packages for some of the elderly people in the nursing home. She was going to need a pair of scissors and a small knife for the activity.

One of the other seventh-graders saw the knife in her backpack and reported it to the teacher. The knife and scissors were confiscated and Sheila has been escorted to the office, where she is waiting for you.

The actions of both of these children fall under the zero tolerance policy of the school district. This policy states that possession of a dangerous weapon is cause for expulsion from school.

Are you starting to feel apprehensive about dealing with these two very different situations even though your course of action is already spelled out in the school discipline plan? Are you starting to think that your decision in this matter is going to be the headline story in the newspaper? Can you already visualize your picture on the front page of a national magazine? Are you thinking about how much fun the media are going to have with the story, "Local Principal Expels Child Planning Humanitarian Project"? Nobody looks forward to looking like the village idiot.

If I were the principal, I would probably think to myself, "Now, this is a no-brainer. I need to come down hard on Judy for intent to do bodily injury, and impose a lighter sentence on Sheila. But I'd hate to have to punish Sheila at all given that she had the knife in her backpack for humanitarian reasons, namely helping the elderly. But then I need to remember that some kind of statement has to be made to the student body about bringing potentially dangerous objects into the school.

"But wait," I'd say to myself. "Who do I think I am? I'm not supposed to think in these situations. We have a district policy that governs my actions. Expulsion is the prescribed consequence for possession of a dangerous weapon."

If I were in this situation, commonly referred to as *between a rock and a hard place,* I'd be saying to myself, "If I apply the *Five Critical Disciplinary Considerations* to each of these situations, there is no way that I can justify expelling both students. My following the prescribed policy is going to be grossly unfair and I am going to look like the village idiot.

"If I don't follow the district's prescribed policy of zero tolerance for weapons, I'm going to have a lot of people on my back complaining about my actions not being consistent with district policy. Failure to adhere to the district policy constitutes insubordination. It's a lose/lose proposition. I want to go hide in the nearest hole."

When we apply the *Five Critical Disciplinary Considerations* we see that in Judy's situation several of the considerations apply. There is evidence of a threat. There is intention to do harm. And we have a child who is upset and angry. But when we look at Jan's situation we see that only one of the five considerations apply, namely that she was in possession of the knife. It doesn't take a clinical wizard to see the silliness in zero tolerance policies and prescriptive discipline plans.

Dealing with Parental Misunderstanding Regarding Individualized Discipline

Suppose I decide to individualize the discipline in these cases. Is it possible that one of these parents will complain? Sure it is. Judy's mother will probably say, "But Sheila did the same thing. She brought a knife to school. She should have received the same punishment. It's not fair for her to get out of this with less punishment. You should treat everyone the same."

Think of it the other way. If I were to follow the plan calling for prescribed discipline, both children would receive the same punishment. Now, Judy's mom would probably not be the one complaining about Sheila getting more lenient treatment. But instead, it would be Sheila's mom arguing that her child should not have received the same punishment as Judy since her circumstances were different. I can't win.

But if I choose to individualize the discipline, and Judy gets a more severe punishment while Sheila gets a less severe punishment, at least I have justification for my actions. I can explain my application of the

Five Critical Disciplinary Considerations. Sheila received a different consequence because her intent was different. There was no evidence of her being upset with other students, and there were no threats of bodily injury.

Of course I am not naïve enough to believe that this explanation will make Judy's mom happy. My many years in the school system taught me that solid facts and good reasons seldom satisfy parents who are determined to stand up for their children. However, knowing that I make decisions based on a thoughtful analysis of the situation makes it possible to look in the mirror the next morning and say, *"You did the best you could, even though there's no guarantee that it will make everyone happy."*

A School Discovers a Better Kind of Discipline Plan

I met two kids outside the front door of one of our local schools. Curious about why they were standing outside during instruction time, I asked why they weren't in class.

"We got kicked out of school, man. We're waiting for our moms to pick us up."

"Wow, that's a real bummer, guys."

"Yeah, this is the strictest school we've ever been at. We been in eight different schools and we never saw a school as strict as this."

"Well, then, I bet you're glad you're going home."

"Naw, man. We don't wanna go home. We like it here."

"You don't want to go home? You said that this is the strictest school you've ever been at. Wouldn't you rather be over at Lincoln Park hanging out with your pals?"

"Naw, man. We like it here. The teachers are cool, and they miss us when we're gone, and they try to help us stay out of trouble, and they're real sad when we do bad stuff. We'd rather hang out here."

I was amazed to hear this and was anxious to visit with the principal to find out how she had created a school that was strict but loving at the same time.

This wise principal was more than happy to tell me that she and the staff had turned the school around with a limited number of rules and a limited number of disciplinary techniques.

"We decided that it was impossible to get all the teachers to react to misbehavior in exactly the same way. Our old discipline plan spelled out exactly what was to be done for each offense. The teachers had been trying be consistent like this for years without results."

She went on to add, "The only result I could see was that it tended to make staff members unhappy with each other for not following the plan as prescribed. And it caused many problems when the prescribed consequences didn't seem to fit a child's particular offense. The staff kept demanding more rules and tougher consequences.

"Fortunately we found something we could all agree on. We could agree on some basic core beliefs about discipline. We could agree on the results we wanted to achieve when working with misbehaving kids. After several sessions we were able to agree on a list of core beliefs that guide our decisionmaking."

Love and Logic Core Beliefs: When Disciplinary Action Is Needed

1. Every attempt will be made to maintain the dignity and self-respect of both the student and the teacher.
2. Students will be guided and expected to solve their problems, or the ones they create, without creating problems for anyone else.
3. Students will be given opportunities to make decisions and live with the consequences, be they good or bad.
4. Misbehavior will be handled with natural or logical consequences instead of punishment, whenever possible.
5. Misbehavior will be viewed as an opportunity for individual problem solving and preparation for the real world as opposed to a personal attack on school or staff.
6. Students will be encouraged to request a "due process" hearing whenever consequences appear to be unfair.
7. School problems will be handled by school personnel. Criminal activity will be referred to the proper authorities.

"Once we developed our core beliefs we posted the list everywhere in the school. The parents received copies as well. The next step in the process was to give staff members permission to handle each disciplinary situation in their own way as long as their actions were consistent with our core beliefs.

"My job as principal was to help teachers look at their own practices and relate them to the core beliefs. It was difficult at times because we soon found that behavior charts, warnings, detention, threats, putting names on the board, and other traditional methods were not consistent with our core beliefs.

"Fortunately I had been introduced to *9 Essential Skills for the Love and Logic Classroom*. This is a training program that we could run and study in our own school. With the help of the Love and Logic Institute, I set the class up in a way where people could earn college credit.

"All of our staff members were given an opportunity to receive this training, which gave them disciplinary skills consistent with our core beliefs. I was careful not to mandate the use of these skills. However, I did mandate that each staff member learn them. During the first half of the year most of the staff experimented with some of the essential skills for creating a Love and Logic classroom."

Essential Skills

Neutralizing Arguing. Teachers had posters in their room that listed appointment times for arguing. "I argue at 12:00 or 3:15 daily, your choice." When students tried to argue, the teachers would just point to the poster, smile, and ask, "When do I argue? Thank you." If kids persisted, the teachers would play "broken record." The principal said that it was amazing to hear the teachers brag about how much more time they had for teaching, and how much energy they had left over at the end of the day.

Anticipatory Consequencing. Teachers learned to deal with discipline on their own terms and on their own time schedule by delaying consequences for misbehavior. They learned to say, "I'll need to do something about that behavior, but not right now. I'll get back to you. Try not to worry about it in the meantime." Putting the situation on hold gave them time to cool down, get advice from other teachers, and get support from the principal before reacting. Anticipatory consequences give the adult the opportunity to anticipate the reaction of the child to possible consequences, and give the child time to stew about the problem.

Short-Term Recovery. Instead of giving warnings or threats, and instead of sending children to the office for discipline for classroom disruptions, the teachers set up several different places where students could go to cool down, or get themselves back together. Each teacher had a place in the room where a student could have no visual contact with others. At the first indication of a disruption the student was asked, "Can you get it together or do you need a little recovery time? If you go to recovery, come back just as soon as you can. We want you back with us. Thank you."

The other Short-Term Recovery stations included:

A Recovery Chair just inside the door of another classroom. This was for children who needed a different location for a short time. It was not intended for discipline.

A Principal's Recovery Chair in a place that did not allow the child to observe the activities of office personnel.

The In-School Suspension Room was changed to a Recovery Room. This was a place where students could go to "recover," but was not for discipline. No classwork was taken to this area. The student's job was to get him- or herself together and return to the classroom as soon as possible. An adult was there only to provide causal supervision.

The principal agreed with the teachers that students who could not get themselves back together in these situations could spend the rest of the day in At-Home Recovery.

"The results were amazing," said the principal. "Office referrals for discipline dropped by over fifty percent. I was sold and so was the staff. By the end of the year I realized that we were all having more fun working with the kids. Staff morale was up, and better yet, I found that the teachers were no longer complaining that they weren't getting enough administrative support."

I asked this wise principal, "Didn't the teachers find this different approach threatening at first? Change is difficult for most people. How did you deal with those who were resistant to the change?"

She responded, "Oh, I didn't tell them that they had to throw away their old discipline plans and techniques. They could keep these in place to provide themselves a security blanket. I only asked them to *experiment* with the new techniques first, and if they didn't work, they could fall back on their old ways. I also told them that I would be asking them, from time to time, to prove to me how the old techniques were consistent with our core beliefs.

"You need to know," she added, "that there are some other benefits derived from our new approach. We have fewer parent complaints, and parent/teacher conferences are much easier. I attribute it to parents being much more aware of how we are trying to work with their children.

"Each parent conference starts with a review of our core beliefs. Teachers ask the parents if any of these beliefs present problems. An agreement is made that any decision made during the conference will be consistent with the beliefs. It's amazing how much better a conference goes when we have a point of common agreement to launch the discussion."

I left the school saying to myself, "I've just witnessed a great example of quality leadership. Every person in this school, both adult and child, profits from this kind of leadership."

Sample School Discipline Plan
Expectations and Rules for Student Conduct

Standards of Student Safety and Security

The school board has set forth rules and expectations addressing student safety and security. Much like the rules that govern our cities, violations of these rules carry penalties, fines, and consequences that are prescribed by law. The purpose of penalties under these federal, state, and local laws is to ensure an orderly and safe society.

The board of education sets the standards for safety and security and has set penalties for violation of these standards. These standards address the safety and security of both children and school staff. They are not up for interpretation at the local school level, just as the laws for our state, county, and city are not up for interpretation or revision by local school administrators.

District Rules

(Fill in this section with a copy of your district rules.)

The penalties or consequences for violating these rules cannot be excused or changed by local school administrators or staff.

Safety and Security Rules

(Fill in this section with your school district document regarding rights, responsibilities, rules, etc. This document usually includes, but is not limited to, the following:)

Possession or use of illegal drugs
Possession or use of alcohol
Acts or threats of violence
Possession of weapons
Possession or use of dangerous articles
Acts or threats of bullying
Acts or threats of sexual harassment
Use and misuse of district facilities and equipment
Use and misuse of the Internet

LOVE AND LOGIC INSTITUTE, INC. 800-338-4065

Penalties for Violation of District Rules

(Fill in this section with a copy of the penalties regarding violation of your district rules.)

School Rules

Safety and Security Rules

All district rules related to safety and security rules are in effect at all times at the local school level.

Rules and Expectations Supporting the Orderly Operation of the School and the Educational Process

Rules and expectations covered in this section are designed to meet the following goals:

1. Maintain an orderly school operation.
2. Maintain optimal learning opportunities for students. School facilities and classrooms must be free of behaviors that interfere with teaching and learning.
3. Help students develop skills and behaviors necessary for healthy social interaction, both present and future.
4. Help students learn how their decisions affect the quality of their lives and the lives of others.
5. Help students develop responsibility and character.

Love and Logic Rules for Our School

1. Treat others with the same respect with which you are treated by the adults in this school.
2. Your actions, dress, possessions, etc., may not cause a problem for anyone else.

Problem actions include, but are not limited to:
(Fill in this section as needed.)

Problems related to dress include, but are not limited to:
(Fill in this section as needed.)

Problems related to possessions include, but are not limited to:
(Fill in this section as needed.)

3. If your actions, dress, or possessions cause a problem for anyone else, you will be asked to solve that problem.

4. If you cannot or choose not to solve the problem, appropriate consequences will be imposed by staff members. These consequences will depend upon the situation and the person or persons involved. Staff members will use their best judgment based upon the information they have at the time.

5. If students and/or parents feel that the consequences appear not to be fair, request a "due process" hearing. A due process hearing does not need to be formal in nature. It is simply a time for concerned individuals to meet together and share information related to the situation in question. In the event that this discussion provides additional information that sheds different light on the situation, or shows the consequences to be unfair, the consequences may be changed or eliminated to better fit the unique situation.

LOVE AND LOGIC INSTITUTE, INC. 800-338-4065

Core Beliefs That Guide Enforcement of School Rules and Expectations

Each student is a unique individual with unique personal, social, and educational needs. As a result, every disciplinary situation becomes unique in nature. Consequences for misbehavior provide the best learning value when matched to the unique student and the unique situation. The odds for children learning from their mistakes increase dramatically when children see a reasonable connection between their behavior and the resulting consequences.

Our school staff dedicates itself to following a set of core beliefs that provide a guide for dealing with student discipline. These core beliefs guide our attempts to individualize disciplinary procedures and to help students see reasonable connections between their behavior and the resulting consequences.

Since these core beliefs provide the guiding light for our professional decisions, the staff encourages parents to bring concerns and questions to us in the event we operate in ways that appear to be inconsistent with these core beliefs.

Love and Logic Core Beliefs for Our School

The following list of core beliefs outlines the professional actions and attitudes of all staff members in this school:

1. Every attempt will be made to maintain the dignity and self-respect of both the student and the teacher.
2. Students will be guided and expected to solve their problems, or the ones they create, without creating problems for anyone else.
3. Students will be given opportunities to make decisions and live with the consequences, be they good or bad.
4. Misbehavior will be handled with natural or logical consequences instead of punishment, whenever possible.
5. Misbehavior will be viewed as an opportunity for individual problem solving and preparation for the real world as opposed to a personal attack on school or staff.

6. Students are encouraged to request a "due process" hearing whenever consequences appear to be unfair.

7. School problems will be handled by school personnel. Criminal activity will be referred to the proper authorities.

Individual Classroom Rules

1. Treat me, as your teacher, with the same respect with which I treat you.

2. Your actions may not cause a problem for anyone else.

3. If you cause a problem, you will be asked to solve it.

4. If you cannot solve the problem or choose not to, I will do something. What I do will depend upon the situation and the person involved.

5. If I do something that appears to be unfair, whisper to me, "I'm not sure that's fair," and we will talk about it.

Helping Parents Understand a Love and Logic Discipline Plan

This chapter is not about how to make sure all parents are happy with your school. There is no end to the documentation about what happens when we try to make everybody happy.

The purpose of this chapter is to show how your staff can clearly define how your school does business and works with kids, so that the healthiest parents, who, by the way, are too busy creating healthy families to be overly critical of the school, understand how much you care about their kids. And it is about helping the unhealthy parents get a view of health, even if they don't like it.

What happens when any group lacks leadership, be it a business, country, family, or any other organization? Chaos! Throughout history we have learned that humans yearn for firm and fair leadership. Studies about why kids seek out gang affiliation tell us that failure to find fair leadership in the families drives kids to find it in gangs. Even though that leadership may not be very democratic, it is strong and provides a sense of security.

When schools try to make everybody happy, there is a lack of willingness and ability to lead in a fair way. In the resulting chaos all the subgroups of the school community are fighting for control. This is no different than what happens in a family when parents fail to be strong role models: the child subconsciously thinks, "If they aren't going to be in control, somebody's going to have to be. I guess it will have to be me." Everyone is aware of the kinds of family disasters that can result.

This is why schools that are afraid to take a stand have students who are misbehaving to establish control, parent groups who are fighting, and disgruntled staff who are arguing and complaining about each other.

We at the Love and Logic Institute have watched, with dismay, the growing national trend for schools to be all things to all people. Delegating professional decisions to those not properly trained for them is not something leaders of other professions would ever consider, let alone do. Yet this is exactly what happens when schools fail to clearly state how they do business and why they do it. If this approach to educating our youth had merit, it would surely have worked by now and there would be no need for this book.

Am I suggesting that parents should not be involved in their schools? Certainly not. Everyone in the community should play a role in helping to establish goals and desired outcomes.

Parents need to be highly involved in helping staff understand specific needs of their own children, and the school staff needs to be equally enthusiastic about listening and designing ways to meet individual needs when appropriate. Good leaders actively involve the community in these areas. The purpose of this chapter is not to eliminate the voice of parents, but to help you develop a process that does not confuse the role of the professional educators and the role of the community.

Bringing Parents On Board

As your school moves toward a principles-based approach to individualizing discipline, parents need to have a clear picture of the school's motives and the approach to be used when there are problems.

Step One
Develop a set of core beliefs for your school or adopt the Love and Logic Core Beliefs found in Chapter 7.

Step Two
Use all available methods to acquaint the school community with your school's core beliefs.

Step Three
Develop and distribute your schoolwide discipline policy.

Step Four
Teachers send a letter, similar to the following sample, to the students' parents, describing the classroom rules and how discipline will be handled.

Sample Letter
The letter presented on the next page, prepared by a Love and Logic teacher, is one of the best examples I know of for sharing this information with parents. Even though this book is protected by copyright, the letter is not. The author of this letter has provided a written release so that it may be copied and used as is, or with modification.

As you study this letter you will note that it provides what is the essence of a "due process" hearing for students or parents who feel that a teacher's decisions are not fair.

The Supreme Court of our country is willing to render new decisions in some cases. Under what conditions will the Court do this? When there is new information. If this is good enough for the Supreme Court, it's good enough for me. Parents who know that this opportunity exists are less likely to attack the school or the teacher as a way to get a decision reviewed.

I first met Amy Kochmal, the author of this letter, when her principal brought her to one of Love and Logic's national conferences. Her principal introduced her like this: "Jim, I want you to meet Amy. I brought her to the conference as a reward. She taught for a whole year without my hearing a parent complaint."

After reading this letter, I bet you'll have a good idea why the principal was not burdened with parent complaints. First of all, the parents knew that there was an avenue for their concerns. And second, they had a clear picture of her motives and her intended ways of working with their kids. Amy provided leadership for both her students and their parents.

GUIDELINES AND CODE OF ETHICS FOR DISCIPLINE
Mrs. Kochmal 1996–97

Rules in my classroom are few. I believe that all children are different, and all actions and reactions very personal in nature. Effective discipline involves a few overriding tenets rather than a long list of specific rules. Situations are dealt with as they arise, with the focus on enabling the child to grow and learn from his or her actions.

Guidelines for Student Behavior

1. You may engage in any behavior which does not create a problem for you or anyone else in the world.
2. If you find yourself with a problem, you may solve it by any means which does not cause a problem for anyone else in the world.
3. You may engage in any behavior that does not jeopardize the safety or learning of yourself or others. Unkind words and actions will not be tolerated.

In ensuring that the above guidelines are adhered to, I will operate with the following principles as my guide:

1. I will react without anger or haste to problem situations.
2. I will provide consequences that are not punitive but that allow the child to experience the results of a poor choice, enabling him or her to make better choices in the future.
3. I will proceed in all situations with the best interest of the child foremost in my mind—academic, social, and emotional well-being will be fostered.
4. I will guide students toward personal responsibility and the decision-making skills they will need to function in the real world.
5. I will arrange consequences for problem situations in such a way that the child will not be humiliated or demeaned.

6. Equal is not always fair. Consequences will be designed to fit the problems of individual students, and they may be different even when problems appear to be the same.

7. I will make every effort to ensure that, in each situation, the students involved understand why they are involved in consequences.

8. If I at any time act or react in a way that a child truly feels is unjust, that student need only say to me, "I'm not sure that's fair." I will arrange a private conference during which the student can express to me why he or she feels my actions were not fair. This may or may not change my course of action. I am always open to calm, rational discussion of any matter.

Step Five

Teachers provide direct instruction to introduce their students to the classroom rules, giving special attention to treating students as unique individuals. Kids who feel good about how they are treated in the classroom can be your best public relations ambassadors.

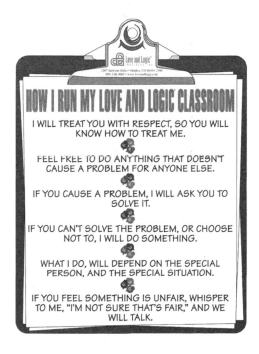

Here is a typical teacher rules presentation (wise teachers adapt the language and vocabulary to fit the age and maturity level of the students):

TEACHER: "Look up here on the wall. This chart tells about the classroom rules. What does it say that I will do if you cause a problem?"

CLASS: "It says that you will ask us to solve it."

TEACHER: "Yes. And does that mean that you are going to need to find a way to make it right in some way?"

CLASS: "Yes."

TEACHER: "And what does it say that I will do if you can't or won't do that?"

CLASS: "It says that you'll do something."

TEACHER: "What does that mean?"

CLASS: (Shrugs and "I don't knows" are the usual response.)

TEACHER: "It means that I'll figure out a consequence or punishment that seems to fit. Now, what do you suppose that means? Does it mean that everybody here gets the same punishment, or does it mean that I'm going to treat you all differently?"

CLASS: "Differently?"

TEACHER: "You bet. I treat everybody differently because why? Is everybody the same, or is everybody different?"

CLASS: "Different."

TEACHER: "Right. And is every situation the same, or is every situation different?"

CLASS: "Different."

TEACHER: "Right. So how am I going to treat everybody and every situation?"

CLASS: "Differently."

TEACHER: "Differently. You bet. Now, here's the problem. Sometimes my consequences are not fair. Sometimes it's because I don't totally understand the situation or have all the facts. Now, look at the chart again. What does it say for you to do if you think one of my decisions is not fair?"

CLASS: "It says to come to you, whisper that we don't think it's fair."

TEACHER: "Right. And if you can present a good case, I'll change the consequence so that it fits better. Now, think about this: What will work best for you? Will it work best to tell your parents that I'm not fair, or would it be better to tell me?"

CLASS: "Tell you?"

TEACHER: "Right. Now does that mean that I'll be mad if you tell your folks, or does it mean that you'll just have to wait longer to get things straightened out? And tell me, what's best for kids, to learn to stand up for themselves, or to depend on parents to do it?"

CLASS: "Do it ourselves."

TEACHER: "You've got that right. Good luck and thank you. I hope this helps."

I have known teachers to actually sign and date the sentence on the chart guaranteeing a due process hearing, saying, "Class, look. Here is my written guarantee to you that if you can present a good case, I will change the consequences to fit better." In front of the class, the teacher signs the chart and says, "There it is, signed and dated."

Step Six
Be prepared for some parents to want their children to know prescribed consequences. These are the parents who look for legal technicalities to excuse their children from being held accountable for their misbehavior.

One of the frequent concerns expressed by school staff is the parental concern about warnings. This is to be expected. It is common for ineffective parents to provide warnings such as:

"You be in on time tonight, or you're going to be grounded."
"If you bring home another bad report card, you're not driving."
"If you say that one more time, you're going to be sorry."

We've all heard these. It appears that many parents actually think that these threats and warnings actually work, but we have learned that this is as ineffective as fighting forest fires with squirt guns. One of the sad but slightly humorous realities is that parents who can make warnings and threats at home often insist that the school use the same useless techniques.

Here is a common response that a parent like this gives the teacher upon discovering that his or her child is subject to a disciplinary action:

PARENT: "It's not fair. You didn't warn him that he would have to experience that kind of punishment."

The most effective technique for dealing with this involves three steps.

1. *Collect information without defending, explaining, or reasoning with the parent.*

"This sounds important. Tell me more."

2. *Prove that you have heard the parent and check for understanding.*

"Let's see if I've got it.

These first two steps are designed to help the parent move from the emotional state to the thinking state. People who are upset operate out of "flight or fight" defensive mode. Listening without debating can help a person change brain chemistry, thus allowing them to move into the thinking state.

3. *Check for entry into the thinking state.*
The best way to discover if a person has entered the thinking state is to ask this benign question:

"Would you like my thoughts?"

People who have entered the thinking state are usually tempted to say, "I guess so." People who are still in the defensive state continue to explain why they are angry.

Applying this technique, let's observe the interchange between the upset parent and the teacher. Here is a step-by-step process:

1. Collecting information without reacting.

PARENT: "It's just not fair. You should have warned him that he'd get that kind of punishment. You have no right to spring this on him."

TEACHER: "I can see that this is upsetting. Tell me more."

PARENT: "Well, at his last school, the kids knew exactly what was going to happen if they acted up. Then the kids knew not to get in trouble."

TEACHER: "Are you saying that kids act better when they are warned?"

PARENT: "Well, I'd certainly think so. That's how we do it at home."

TEACHER: "Tell me more about that."

PARENT: "We let him know, in no uncertain terms, that if he acts up he's going to be grounded. That's how my parents did it and I turned out just fine. You guys are too easy on these kids and then you get all over their cases. It's just not fair."

TEACHER: "So, tell me how this works. Does this usually work to get him to do what you want?"

PARENT: "Well, he knows he's going to be in big trouble if he doesn't."

2. Proving that you've heard the parent and understood.

TEACHER: "Let's see if I've got it. You say that we're not fair by punishing him without warning him? You're saying that he'd probably behave if we warned him? You're saying that he wouldn't be in trouble if we did that? Is there anything I've missed?"

PARENT: "That's what I'm talking about. That's how my school ran when I was a kid."

3. *Checking for the parent's entry into the thinking state.*

It is important to remember that people will not listen until they feel like they have been heard.

TEACHER: "Would you like my thoughts?"

PARENT: "I guess so."

TEACHER: "We used to warn kids of the exact consequences they would face if they broke the rules. In fact, schools did that for many, many years. It just didn't work. This school is different because we try to treat each kid like a unique individual. We know that each situation is different, each kid is different, and that consequences must be different to fit the kid and the situation. We tell the kids that if they break the rules we will do something that we think will fit the situation. If you check out our discipline policy, we also give kids and their parents a chance to tell their side of the story in case we have made a wrong decision based on not having enough information. If kids can present a good case, we are willing to change the consequence so that it fits better. I even taught the kids how to do this so they didn't have to be afraid to let me know if my actions weren't fair. Why do you suppose that he didn't do that, but came to you instead?"

PARENT: "Well, I guess he doesn't feel comfortable doing that."

TEACHER: "That's really sad. I'd like to work with him to help him feel more comfortable. Do you have some thoughts about that?"

Notice that this teacher was not defensive. A Love and Logic school discipline plan provides the flexibility to do what is right for each child, and this step-by-step technique for dealing with an upset parent offers up a win/win situation for child, parent, and teacher.

Nine Essential Skills for a Classroom Teacher

ESSENTIAL SKILL NUMBER ONE
Neutralizing Student Arguing

Step One: Go brain dead.

Remember: There is nothing wrong with a kid that a little reasoning won't make worse. Never attempt to reason with the child. Don't attempt to explain your position. Logic does not work in these situations because the child is playing by a different set of rules than you are. He or she is not interested in facts and logic, but in seeing you give up.

Step Two: Choose a Love and Logic "one-liner" antidote.

"I respect you too much to argue."
"I bet it feels that way."
"I know."
"How sad."

"Nice try."

"Thanks for noticing that."

"What a bummer."

"Could be."

Step Three: Do not attempt to think.

Become a "broken record," saying the same antidote for each new argument the youngster comes up with. Keep your voice soft. Allow any frustration to be that of the child, not of you.

Step Four: If the child continues to argue ...

For some very strong-willed or manipulative children, it is effective to say, "I argue at 12:15 or 3:15 daily. What would be best for you?" And then play "broken record" with this question. Don't give in to the temptation to match wits with a child.

ESSENTIAL SKILL NUMBER TWO
Delayed Consequence

Immediate consequences work really well with rats,
pigeons, mice, and monkeys.
In real-world classrooms, they typically create more
problems than they solve.

Problems with Immediate Consequences

1. Most of us have great difficulty thinking of one while we are teaching.
2. We "own" the problem rather than hand it back to the child. In other words, we are forced to do more thinking than the child.
3. We are forced to react while we and the child are upset.
4. We don't have time to anticipate how the child, his or her parents, our administrators, and others will react to our response.
5. We don't have time to put together a reasonable plan and a support team to help us carry it out.
6. We often end up making threats we can't back up.
7. We generally fail to deliver a strong dose of empathy before providing the consequence.
8. Every day we live in fear that some kid will do something that we won't know how to handle with an immediate consequence.

Take care of yourself, and give yourself a break! Here's how:

The next time a student does something inappropriate, experiment with saying,

Oh, no. This is sad. I'm going to have to do something about this!
But not now ... later. Try not to worry about it.

With a very explosive student it is probably wiser to say nothing to him or her until you have a plan and the situation is safe.

The delayed or "anticipatory" consequence allows you time to anticipate whose support you might need, how the child might try to react, and how to make sure that you can actually follow through with a logical consequence. This technique also allows the child to anticipate or worry about a wide array of possible consequences.

The anticipatory consequence technique gains its power from this basic principle of conditioning: When one stimulus consistently predicts a second, the first stimulus gains the same emotional properties as the second. Stated simply: When "try not to worry about it" consistently predicts something the child really must worry about, "try not to worry about it" becomes a consequence in and of itself—an anticipatory consequence.

ESSENTIAL SKILL NUMBER THREE
Empathy

Some Benefits of Delivering Consequences with Empathy

1. The child is not distracted by the adult's anger.
2. The child must "own" his or her pain rather than blaming it on the adult.
3. The adult-child relationship is maintained.
4. The child is much less likely to seek revenge.
5. The adult is seen as being able to handle problems without breaking a sweat.
6. The child learns through modeling to use empathy with others.

Keep your empathy short, sweet, simple, and repetitive.

Most adults find it difficult to deliver empathy when a child has misbehaved. The more natural tendency is to show anger, threaten, and lecture. Teachers generally find it much easier to pick one or two simple empathic responses to repeat over and over with their students. When students hear these same statements repeated, they learn two things:

1. The teacher cares about them.
2. The teacher is not going to back down. No use in arguing!

A Menu of Empathic Responses

"This must really hurt."
"This is so sad."
"This is really hard."
"Bummer."
"I'm sorry you feel so bad."
"It must be hard to feel that way."

The Power of Nonverbal Communication

Studies estimate that 70–90 percent of what we communicate, we do without words through subtle nonverbal gestures. Research also reveals that students are experts at decoding these nonverbal cues.

When delivering empathic responses, the delivery is as important as your actual words: Avoid sarcasm at all costs!

ESSENTIAL SKILL NUMBER FOUR
The Recovery Process

The Pyramid of Short-Term Recovery Settings

The Pyramid of Short-Term Recovery Settings is a technique designed to preserve the learning environment in your classroom when specific students are becoming disruptive. ***This tool is not intended to be punitive or humiliating.*** Each alternative setting merely represents a place where a student can go *temporarily* with the goal of eliminating the disruption—so that you can continue teaching. As one moves up the pyramid, the settings become progressively more restrictive. Generally, teachers are advised to start near the bottom and move up only as needed. With more severe disruptive behavior, a teacher may need to start at a higher level. Below is an example of the settings included in a typical pyramid.

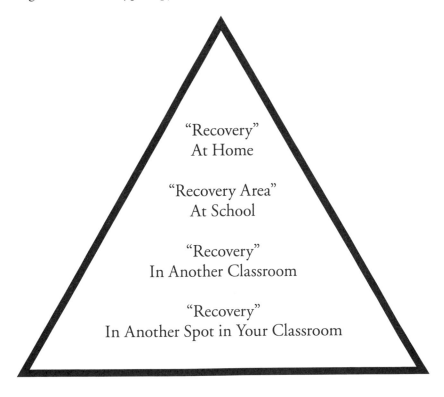

"Recovery"
At Home

"Recovery Area"
At School

"Recovery"
In Another Classroom

"Recovery"
In Another Spot in Your Classroom

There are eight basic questions that must be answered before using this technique. Careful planning to answer the following questions is essential!

1. What settings are appropriate for our unique school?
2. When should a student be sent to an alternative setting?
3. How should the student be sent?
4. What should the student do in this setting?
5. How long should the student stay in the setting?
6. What should a teacher do if the student resists going?
7. Have we included administrators and parents in our planning?
8. What legal and ethical issues are involved?

1. What settings are appropriate for our unique school?

Try to develop a full range of settings, from minimally restrictive to very restrictive. The students should be supervised but receive minimal attention. It is also helpful to have multiple alternative classrooms to use so that a student is not sent to the same room each time and so multiple students can be removed if necessary.

2. When should a student be sent to an alternative setting?

A student should be sent when other preventative measures have not been successful and they are interfering with the learning of others. A student should not be removed merely for not doing his or her work.

3. How should the student be sent?

Whispering a choice to the student such as, "Can you stay with us or do you need to leave?" or whispering, "There's a seat for you in Ms. Smith's room," is often effective. The goal should be to avoid embarrassing the student and to use empathy.

4. What should the student do in this setting?

The student should not be asked to complete work or receive counseling. He or she should get minimal attention when in the setting. Counseling should be saved for later, when the student is calm and well behaved.

5. How long should the student stay in the setting?

The student should stay just long enough to get calmed down. For more serious misbehavior, the student should have a written plan for how they intend to avoid the problem in the future. For more chronic problems, more restrictive settings may be needed, along with other types of disciplinary and/or mental health interventions.

6. What should a teacher do if the student resists going?

If the student will not go, direct the rest of the class to a different location and have another teacher attempt to remove him or her. If the student continues to resist, the administrators may need to call the police. Do not attempt to physically remove the student!

7. Have we included administrators and parents in our planning?

It is essential that fellow teachers and administrators be involved in planning. Parents should also be aware of the school's policy once it is adopted.

8. What ethical and legal issues are involved?

Special Education Law: PL 105-17 I.D.E.A.

A. Least restrictive environment.

B. IEP ... Is the program individualized and responsive to the child's needs?

C. Parental involvement and other due process requirements.

D. Maximum cumulative suspensions: ten days.

E. Document all of the positive interventions you have used to prevent the child from being removed from your classroom!

Ethical Issues

A. When a child needs constant removal, what is their behavior really saying?

I'm not getting what I really need to be successful.

B. Use of this plan is not an excuse to do nothing to help the child.
C. The child should be involved as much as possible in a plan to prevent frequent use of this approach.
D. Undue humiliation and other punishment must be avoided.
E. *We must continue to show the child that we care!*

ESSENTIAL SKILL NUMBER FIVE
Developing Positive Teacher-Student Relationships

The One-Sentence Intervention

Research clearly shows that the primary element contributing to success with at-risk students is a positive relationship between the student and the teacher. Research also indicates that this relationship is developed most effectively when the teacher displays interest in aspects of the student that are not traditionally school related. That is, this relationship blossoms when the teacher notices and accepts the student as a unique human being—rather than just a pupil.

1. What are the student's nonacademic strengths and interests?
2. List six brief statements you can use to notice these strengths and interests. (Example: "I've noticed that you really like to draw.")

"I've noticed that _____."
"I've noticed that _____."
"I've noticed that _____."
"I've noticed that _____."
"I've noticed that _____."
"I've noticed that _____."

Do not end the statement with something like, "... and that's great!"

3. When and where can you make these statements without embarrassing the student?
4. Which other teachers will help you use this technique with the student?
5. Approach the student, smile, and use the statements identified above at least two times a week for at least three weeks.
6. Listen to the student if he or she wants to talk about the strength or interest.

7. ***Do not use this technique when the student is upset.*** Save it for calm times.

8. When the student is about to do something you don't want, or if you want him or her to do something else, experiment with saying, "Will you do this just for me?" or "Just because I like you, should I let you do this?"

ESSENTIAL SKILL NUMBER SIX
Setting Limits with Enforceable Statements

Limits are set when the adult says:

"This is how I'm going to run my own life."
"I'll be listening to those who raise their hands."

Limits are enforced when the adult does
not engage in arguments about the limits:

"So when will I be glad to listen to you? Thanks."

Turn Your Words Into Gold
The Art of Enforceable Statements for the School

Ineffective Technique	Love and Logic Technique
Please sit down. I'm going to start now.	I'll begin as soon as you are seated.
Please be quiet. It's time to begin.	I'll be glad to start as soon as you show me that you are ready.
Open your books to page 54.	I'll be working from page 54.
I'm not going to line you up until everyone is quiet.	I'll be lining people up as soon as it is quiet.
Don't sharpen your pencil while I'm talking.	I allow people to sharpen pencils when I am not giving directions.
You can't go to the restroom until I finish the directions.	Feel free to go to the restroom when I'm done giving directions.
Don't be bothering your neighbors.	You are welcome to stay with us as long as you and others are not being bothered.
Keep your hands to yourself.	Feel free to stay with us when you can keep your hands to yourself.
Turn your assignment in on time or you'll get a lower grade.	I give full credit for papers turned in on time.
Don't talk to me in that tone of voice!	I'll listen as soon as your voice is as calm as mine.
You show some respect.	I'll be glad to discuss this when respect is shown.
Don't be late for class.	All of those who arrive on time go home on time.
Don't try to turn in sloppy papers to me.	I'll be glad to accept all papers that meet the neatness standard for this room.
Keep your desks organized and neat.	All owners of neat desks are welcome to join us at recess.
I'm not loaning you any more paper.	I loan paper to those who have not borrowed before.
If you can't remember your pencil, you're just going to have to do without.	Feel free to borrow from anyone but me.
You're not going out without your coat.	You may go out as soon as you have your coat.
You're not going to stay in this group and act like that.	You may stay with us if you can give up on that behavior.
Don't you come back to this room until you can show some respect!	Feel free to come back to the room as soon as you are calm.
Quit breaking the rules of this game.	Those who can follow the rules are welcome to play the game.
Get this classroom cleaned up right now, and I mean it!	You are welcome to join us for _____ as soon as the classroom is clean.
Stop arguing with me.	I'll be glad to discuss this with you as soon as the arguing stops.
If you can't treat the paintbrushes right, you'll just have to sit out this project.	All of those who can handle the paintbrushes right are welcome to join us in the project.
If you forget your permission slip, you're going to miss the trip.	All of those who remember permission slips are welcome to go on the field trip.

ESSENTIAL SKILL NUMBER SEVEN
Using Choices to Prevent Power Struggles

Guidelines for Giving Lots of Little Choices

1. Never give a choice on an issue that might cause a problem for you or for anyone else.
2. For each choice, give only two options, each of which will be okay with you.
3. If the child doesn't decide in ten seconds, decide for him or her.
4. Only give choices that fit with your value system.

Some Examples of Little Choices

"Should this paper be due on Wednesday or Thursday?"

"Feel free to do the first half of this assignment or the second half."
   (Be sure to give an assignment that is twice as long as you want.)

"Feel free to do this in pen or pencil."

"We are going on a field trip in six months. Would you like to go to the zoo or the museum of natural history?"

"Would you like to go to recess on-time or late?"

"Can you stay with us and stop that, or do you need to leave for a while and come back when you are calm?"

"Do you want to do this in groups or have me lecture?"

"Feel free to choose where you sit as long as it doesn't cause a problem for anyone else."

"Do the first twenty-five problems or the second twenty-five. You decide."

ESSENTIAL SKILL NUMBER EIGHT
Quick and Easy Preventative Interventions

Here is a list of quick and easy preventative interventions, by degree of severity:

1. Give the student "the evil eye." (Or better yet, a wink and a smile.)
2. Walk toward the student.
3. Stand close to the student.
4. Make eye contact and shake your head indicating "No."
5. Place a gentle hand upon the shoulder of the student.
6. Make a statement indicating disfavor, such as:

   "Really now, Jeff, must you?"
   "Just because I like you, should I let you get by with that?"

7. Change the student's location by asking:

   "Jeff, would you consider moving over here for a minute?"
   "Would you mind waiting here for a minute, and then we can talk?"

8. Make a statement indicating that the behavior is just misplaced (if appropriate):

   "That behavior would be fine on the playground. It isn't okay here."
   "That's not acceptable here."
   "Save it for later."

9. Use an "I Message":

   "I get distracted when there is a pencil tapping."
   "It scares me to see you running in the hall. Wait right here for a
       moment, then you can go."

10. Set limits by describing what you allow, do, or provide, without telling the student what to do about it:

   "I listen to people who raise their hands."
   "I give credit for all papers that are on my desk by 3:15."
   "I'll dismiss people as soon as desks are clean."
   "Feel free to return to the group as soon as you can handle it."

11. Provide choices:

   "Would you rather work quietly with the group or go to recovery?"
   "Would you rather talk this over quietly with me now or after school?"

12. Remove the student from the group to recovery. The student is allowed to return when he or she can live with the limitations of the group or teacher.

13. Require the student to fill in a form during time-out before he or she can return to the group, answering self-questions such as:

   a. What happened?
   b. How did I feel?
   c. What did I do?
   d. How did it work?
   e. What am I going to do next time?

14. Excuse the student to the office for a short "cooling off" period. No counseling is requested of the administrator.

15. Give the student an appointment to talk about the problem. Counseling involves requiring him or her to come up with a new behavior before returning to the scene of the rule violation.

16. Restrict the student from the area of his or her infraction until a new plan of action is identified and written out by the student.

17. Restrict the student from the area of the infraction until the adults

feel that another try is in order. The student may then return to the area on a day-to-day basis:

"You may start using the playground again. Each good day you have earns you another day."

18. Provide a natural or logical consequence with empathy:

"I'm sorry it worked out that way for you. Where are you going to eat now that you can't eat in the cafeteria? It has to be a place that won't be a problem for anyone else. Think it over and let me know."

19. Have the student make an "informational telephone call" to his or her parents describing the problem and his or her plans for improvement. The teacher should call first without the student's knowledge to alert the parents and to seek support.
20. Have the student write an "informational letter" to his or her parents describing the problem and including plans for improvement. The letter is to be signed by the parents and returned to the teacher as the student's ticket to rejoin the class.
21. Make an appointment with the administrator for consultation. The teacher, administrator, and student form a team to discuss possible solutions or consequences.
22. Hold a parent conference. This should include the parent, teacher, administrator, and student.
23. Suspend the student from school until a parent conference is held.
24. Place the student on a "systematic suspension" contract, allowing him or her to remain in school each day for as many minutes or hours as the child can abide by an agreed-upon set of behavioral standards.

ESSENTIAL SKILL NUMBER NINE
Guiding Students to Own and Solve Their Problems

Love and Logic Step One: Empathy.

"How sad."
"I bet that hurts."

Love and Logic Step Two: Send the "Power Message."

"What do you think you're going to do?"

Love and Logic Step Three: Offer choices.

"Would you like to hear what other kids have tried?"

At this point, offer a variety of choices that range from bad to good. It's usually best to start out with the poor choices. Each time a choice is offered, go on to step four, forcing the youngster to state the consequence in his or her own words. This means that you will be going back and forth between steps three and four.

Love and Logic Step Four: Have the child state the consequence.

"And how will that work?"

Love and Logic Step Five: Give permission for the child to either solve the problem or not solve the problem.

"Good luck. I hope it works out."

Have no fear. If the child is fortunate enough to make a poor choice, he or she may experience a double learning lesson.

How to Guide a Teacher Toward Creating a Love and Logic Classroom

Would you have more energy at the end of the day if you weren't so frequently pulled into unwinnable battles waged between teachers, their students, and their parents? Would life be less stressful if the teachers in your school had the skills to handle classroom discipline without breaking a sweat?

It doesn't take a brain surgeon to know that life is better for school administrators when life is better for their teachers and their students! Listed below are some tips for guiding a teacher toward developing a positive and practical approach to leading their classroom with Love and Logic.

Make sure that the teacher is ready for Love and Logic.

Don't waste your precious time trying to "convert" the most negative people on your staff! As I often preach, start with the "sponges" in your building—those folks who'll actually soak up the ideas you provide. Unsuccessful administrators start with the "bricks" in their building. They quickly find that bricks just aren't that absorbent!

Some administrators actually decide to make Love and Logic more valuable by holding it back. They create interest by making it harder to get. One administrator put it this way:

At the beginning of the year, I informed my staff that I'd be taking applications for those who wanted to borrow some Love and Logic materials. I let them know that I'd select a few applicants based on who completed the most compelling one-page application letter. Then I simply chose about ten of my most enthusiastic teachers. I lent them the materials, and it wasn't long before they were extremely excited.

I warned these people to keep what they learned "top secret." It's amazing how interest goes up when people think they are missing out on something!

As time passed, I let more lucky folks share in the fun. Before long, most of my staff was on board.

Provide some introductory study materials.

Listed below are some of the materials most loved by teachers new to Love and Logic:

- *Teaching with Love and Logic: Taking Control of the Classroom*
- *Quick and Easy Classroom Interventions: 23 Proven Tools for Increasing Student Cooperation*
- *How to Teach Without Getting Punched: Preventing Battles and Blow-ups with Angry Students*
- *Hope for Underachieving Kids: Opening the Door to Success with Love and Logic*
- *Putting Parents at Ease: Nine Keys to Effective Parent-Teacher Conferences*
- *Calming the Chaos: Behavior Improvement Strategies for the Child with ADHD*
- *9 Essential Skills for the Love and Logic Classroom: Low Stress Strategies for Highly Successful Educators* (training program)

Remind the teacher that successful learning requires plenty of spaced repetition and review.

Common sense coincides with scientific research when it comes to how people learn the best. Repetition and review are the keys! Encourage teachers to expose themselves to the same Love and Logic materials several times. This "overlearning" will enable them more automatically apply the techniques when they are teaching and the heat is on.

Encourage the teacher to start slow by experimenting with one skill at a time.

Three decades of experience has shown that teachers—and parents—are most successful when they start with neutralizing the arguing. When this skill is mastered, additional skills are much easier to implement.

When we use new skills, kids rarely thank us. They argue instead! If we are not prepared for a child's initial reaction to our new skills, we have no new skills.

Wise teachers post a sign in their classroom that reads:

I argue during recess and after school.

After the teacher has put an end to arguing, he or she can begin to experiment with additional skills, one at a time.

Ask the teacher to develop between five and eight Love and Logic principles to guide their disciplinary decisions.

A powerful way of explaining this to teachers is to ask, "If your picture was on the front page of the newspaper, which basic beliefs about classroom discipline would you be proud to have printed next to it?"

After asking this question, provide the teacher with a copy of the handout "Identify the Principles That Guide Your Disciplinary Decisions," found on pages 94–95 of this book.

Ask the teacher to provide you with a copy of the principles he or she selects. Briefly review them to be certain that they are consistent with Love and Logic. Place a copy of these principles in the teacher's file.

Provide the teacher with a copy of the handout "Guidelines and Code of Ethics for Discipline."

Ask the teacher to use the handout, found on pages 51–52 and 88–89 of this book, as a guide in developing his or her own classroom discipline plan. When completed, have the teacher post the plan in the classroom and send a copy to each student's parents.

Give the teacher some quick tips on how to most effectively use their Love and Logic plan.

Tip #1: *Do not warn students about specific consequences in advance!* Just indicate that you will respond to each problem in an individualized manner, depending upon the unique situation.

Tip #2: When making disciplinary decisions, ask yourself, "How is my proposed intervention consistent with my core beliefs? Handle discipline problems in a case-by-case manner, focusing on the unique characteristics of each situation.

Tip #3: If you don't know what to do at any given moment, delay the consequence, refer to your plan, and discuss possible solutions with teachers, administrators, or the child's parents.

Tip #4: Always plug the holes in your plan before carrying it out. Ask, "What might go wrong with this plan?" and fix the potential problems before they happen.

Tip #5: Your goal is to achieve consistency by basing each of your decisions on your set of core principles—rather than trying to treat every problem the same using a "cookbook" approach.

Caution the teacher to avoid the "Consequence Trap."

Research clearly tells us that the most successful teachers use far fewer consequences than the least successful ones. Why is this? Because the most effective teachers focus the vast majority of their energy on developing practical strategies for preventing misbehavior before it happens—or before it intensifies and "infects" other students. The least effective teachers are constantly caught in the trap of trying to find bigger and more unpleasant consequences to throw at kids after they act up.

Dr. Charles Fay (my wise and brilliant son), says it this way:

The most successful teachers focus on prevention.
The least successful ones focus on detention.

Help your teachers understand that developing positive relationships and using other preventative techniques is a far more powerful strategy than waiting for kids to act up—and trying to figure out what type of consequences to provide.

GUIDELINES AND CODE OF ETHICS FOR DISCIPLINE
Mrs. Kochmal 1996–97

Rules in my classroom are few. I believe that all children are different, and all actions and reactions very personal in nature. Effective discipline involves a few overriding tenets rather than a long list of specific rules. Situations are dealt with as they arise, with the focus on enabling the child to grow and learn from his or her actions.

Guidelines for Student Behavior

1. You may engage in any behavior which does not create a problem for you or anyone else in the world.
2. If you find yourself with a problem, you may solve it by any means which does not cause a problem for anyone else in the world.
3. You may engage in any behavior that does not jeopardize the safety or learning of yourself or others. Unkind words and actions will not be tolerated.

In ensuring that the above guidelines are adhered to, I will operate with the following principles as my guide:

1. I will react without anger or haste to problem situations.
2. I will provide consequences that are not punitive but that allow the child to experience the results of a poor choice, enabling him or her to make better choices in the future.
3. I will proceed in all situations with the best interest of the child foremost in my mind—academic, social, and emotional well-being will be fostered.
4. I will guide students toward personal responsibility and the decision-making skills they will need to function in the real world.
5. I will arrange consequences for problem situations in such a way that the child will not be humiliated or demeaned.

6. Equal is not always fair. Consequences will be designed to fit the problems of individual students, and they may be different even when problems appear to be the same.

7. I will make every effort to ensure that, in each situation, the students involved understand why they are involved in consequences.

8. If I at any time act or react in a way that a child truly feels is unjust, that student need only say to me, "I'm not sure that's fair." I will arrange a private conference during which the student can express to me why he or she feels my actions were not fair. This may or may not change my course of action. I am always open to calm, rational discussion of any matter.

Steps for Creating a Love and Logic School

Introduce Love and Logic to your staff.

- Have the staff listen to the first two stories on the CD *Four Steps to Responsibility.* Make the CD available to those who are interested.
- Invite a staff member from a Love and Logic school to make a presentation to your staff.
- Give your staff copies of the free handouts provided at www.loveandlogic.com.
- Invite a consultant from the Love and Logic Institute to make a presentation to the school or the school district. For information on hiring Jim Fay or Dr. Charles Fay, phone 800-424-3630.

Create a Love and Logic study group.

Do not mandate Love and Logic. This group should be made up of volunteers who are the enthusiastic about learning new ways of working with students.

- If possible, provide one hour of release time on a repeated basis for this select group to study the training program *9 Essential Skills for the Love and Logic Classroom.* Have these staff members conduct experiments with the Love and Logic techniques and informally share their enthusiasm for the results. The best results come when the administrator is part of the study group.

- Create additional study groups as more and more staff become interested.
- Set up opportunities for your staff to earn college credit for participation in this study group. For details, phone the Love and Logic Institute at 800-338-4065.
- Provide the same kind of study opportunities for support staff members.

Develop a lending library of training materials.

Visit with our Love and Logic customer service department at 800-338-4065 for suggestions and ideas about the most efficient use of your budget.

Create a buildingwide Love and Logic philosophy of discipline.

Develop an agreed-upon set of basic Love and Logic principles that serve as a guide for all disciplinary interventions. (*Note:* This entire process may take up to a year. Don't rush it. Let it evolve.) Listed below are some suggested steps.

Step 1: Provide each staff member with a copy of the handout "Identify the Principles That Guide Your Disciplinary Decisions," found on pages 94–95 of this book.

Step 2: Ask each staff member to take some time to circle five or six of the Love and Logic values or principles they would be proud to endorse.

Step 3: Encourage faculty members to change the wording of these Love and Logic principles as they see appropriate.

Step 4: Hold grade-level meetings where staff members discuss the Love and Logic principles they circled. Next, use this discussion to develop an agreed-upon set of principles representing the entire grade level. List these Love and Logic principles on paper.

Step 5: Conduct a meeting with teachers from all grade levels. Have the staff vote to select a set of core principles or beliefs. It is important that the vote take place where all staff members can see the results. Use the selected principles to develop a school-wide list of Love and Logic principles.

Step 6: Post these Love and Logic principles in every room of the school.

Step 7: Share this Love and Logic document with parents and other community members, asking for their support in helping the school meet this commitment.

Step 8: When developing Love and Logic disciplinary interventions, ask, "How is my proposed intervention consistent with our overall principles of discipline?"

Step 9: Encourage each staff member to deal with discipline situations in their own unique ways based upon the merits of the situation, provided that the actions taken by the adult are consistent with the posted Love and Logic principles of the schoolwide philosophy.

Get parents on the "same page" by providing Love and Logic parenting classes.

The easiest and most effective way of doing this is by purchasing the program titled *Becoming a Love and Logic Parent*. This program has been designed to be used without prior training. It is very practical and easy to teach. Just follow the simple lesson plans.

Make it available to parents of children of all ages, but consider the parents of preschool and kindergarten children as your primary target audience.

You will find that each parent who takes this course will be much more supportive of the school staff. In just a few short years, you can have the entire community speaking the same language about raising kids. And your job will get a lot easier!

IDENTIFY THE PRINCIPLES THAT GUIDE YOUR DISCIPLINARY DECISIONS

This is a list of common beliefs about discipline. Identify five or six that most accurately describe the principles you hold regarding discipline and working with students. You may need to change some of the wording. Approach this task as though the principles you identify will soon appear beside your name on the front page of the local paper.

1. I believe that students should be guided and expected to solve the problems they create without creating problems for anyone else.
2. I believe that the sooner students learn that adults are the bosses, the better they learn and behave.
3. I believe that students should learn that misbehavior makes adults angry.
4. I believe that I should make every attempt to maintain the dignity of both the student and the adult during a disciplinary situation.
5. I believe that students should expect rewards for good behavior.
6. I believe that students should expect easy consequences for first and second offenses.
7. I believe that students should learn that breaking rules means lost privileges.
8. I believe that students should see a reasonable connection between their actions and the consequences that follow.
9. I believe that students must show respect for adults simply because they are the adults.
10. I believe that students should be given opportunities to make decisions and live with the consequences, be they good or bad.
11. I believe that the adult's emphasis should be placed on helping students learn to problem-solve and to adopt new behaviors, instead of making students "pay" for past misdeeds.
12. I believe that school issues should be handled by school personnel, and that violations of criminal law should be handled by the authorities.

13. I believe that misbehavior should be handled with natural or logical consequences instead of punishment, whenever possible.

14. I believe that students should have an opportunity to invoke a simple "due process" hearing if they believe that consequences are unfair.

15. I believe that students should expect in-school suspension or discipline if they irritate teachers or don't do assignments.

16. I believe that students should know exactly what consequences they will face if they misbehave.

When Students Feed Off Of Each Other

Dealing effectively with this problem requires understanding the following principle:

Group misbehavior begins with *individual* misbehavior.

Group misbehavior starts when an informal group leader begins to act out and "infects" his or her followers. Ending these types of disruptions largely requires building positive alliances with the leaders. Listed below are some ideas.

Step 1: Identify the leader or leaders within the misbehaving group.
  • It can be helpful to rate each student according to his or her degree of "leadership" in the problem. Keep this list private and confidential.

Step 2: Find acceptable ways for these leaders to look good in front of the group.
  • Avoid praising leaders, particularly in front of their followers.
  • Have private conversations with leaders to discuss ways you can avoid embarrassing them in front of their peers.

Step 3: Spend extra time building relationships with these leaders.
- Use the "One-Sentence Intervention." (See page 14 in this book.)
   "I noticed other kids really look up to you."
- Ask the student for help.
   "Would you consider helping me with some of these guys?"

Step 4: When leaders begin to misbehave, intervene quickly.
- Teach with an overhead projector so your back isn't turned.
- Use the assumption of compliance.
   "I don't want to embarrass you. Thanks for stopping."

Step 5: If others join in, divide and conquer using your alternative settings. (See "Essential Skill Number Four: The Recovery Process," found on pages 65–71 in this book.)
- Ask each of the misbehaving students to leave for a while, starting with the most compliant.

Step 6: Have brief one-on-one meetings with the leaders.
- Wonder out loud about why the leader is continuing to misbehave.
   "Some students do this because the teacher embarrassed them."
   "Some do it because life is really horrible at home."
   "Some do it because they want friends so badly."
   "Some do it because they aren't strong enough to control themselves."

Do not expect the student to answer you. And don't answer for the student. Simply say, "I hope you can work this out. Let me know if you want some help."

Remedy for Tardy Students

What Does Not Work

The following have been used for years with little or no positive results:

Punishment
Lectures
Warnings
Sending kids to the office
Rewards
Detention
Suspensions
Keeping kids after school
Taking kids and parents to court

For Best Results

1. Build a positive teacher-pupil relationship so that the student would rather be with the teacher than elsewhere.

2. The first five minutes of class time should be devoted to an exercise for which the student is held accountable. This exercise is one that cannot be made up at a later date. This is a good time for the kids to work with other students to complete an assignment made up of several review questions. This meets some needs of the child, as well as providing valuable reinforcement for learning.

   These assignments must be turned in for points toward the student's grade at a specific time. It is often helpful for students to correct each other's papers to eliminate additional work for the teacher.

3. The teacher stands in front of the classroom door, greeting students and providing the three elements of love:

   Eye contact

   Smiles

   Touch in the form of handshakes, high-fives, etc.

4. The teacher greets students with:

   "Good morning. Good to see you."

   "Good morning. Glad you made it."

   "Good to see you. We missed you yesterday."

In the Event the Student Is Tardy

The teacher moves toward the student, smiles, and says, "I'm glad you made it. I was worried about you."

   Do not reprimand.

   Do not punish.

This is key to the success of this approach, and this is the way it is handled even if the student is extremely late. Sorrow can be expressed for his or her missing of the opening assignment, but the student is never allowed to make up the opening assignment regardless of the value of the excuse. Say, "I'm sorry you missed it, but maybe you'll have a chance to earn some points tomorrow when you get here on time." While the problems associated with tardiness should rest squarely on the shoulder of the person who is tardy, the responsibility of making the first five minutes of class time too valuable for a student to miss should rest squarely on the shoulder of the teacher. Involving other staff members such as counselors, administrators, etc., is a waste of valuable time and money; I have rarely seen this be to effective in cases of tardiness.

5. Kids who continue to have problems with being late are probably indicating that something is going wrong in their lives and need to have the teacher spend some time working with them. This time should be spent in problem solving rather than in a punitive way. The ultimate solution will come through the relationship the teacher builds with the student, not through punitive measures.

A school is not a prison!

Index

Love and Logic Seminars

Jim Fay and Charles Fay, Ph.D., present
Love and Logic seminars and personal
appearances for both parents and educators
in many cities each year.

For more information contact the
Love and Logic Institute at:

800-424-3630

or visit our website:

www.loveandlogic.com